ELISENDA CASTELLS / GABRIELLE MURPHY

Seek & Find
BIBLE

LOYOLAPRESS.

Old Testament

- The Creation Story, 4
- Adam and Eve, 6
- Building the Ark, 8
- The Great Flood, 10
- Abraham and Sarah, 12
- Isaac, 14
- Jacob's Dream, 16
- Jacob's Children, 18
- Joseph, 20
- Joseph and His Brothers, 22
- Joseph in Egypt, 24
- The Israelites in Egypt, 26
- Moses, 28
- The Burning Bush, 30
- Leaving Egypt, 32
- A Path Through the Water, 34
- Manna from Heaven, 36
- The Ten Commandments, 38
- The Ark of the Covenant, 40
- David and Goliath, 42
- King David in Jerusalem, 44
- Solomon, the Wise King, 46
- Daniel and the Lions, 48
- The Prophet Jonah, 50
- The Prophet Isaiah, 52

- An Angel Visits Mary, 54
- Mary Visits Elizabeth, 56
- The Birth of Jesus, 58
- The Adoration of the Shepherds, 60
- The Magi, 62
- Jesus in the Temple, 64
- The Baptism of Jesus, 66
- Jesus' Disciples, 68
- The Wedding at Cana, 70
- The Sermon on the Mount, 72
- Multiplication of the Loaves and Fish, 74
- The Parables, 76
- The Lost Sheep, 78
- Jesus and the Children, 80
- Triumphal Entry into Jerusalem, 82
- Judas's Betrayal, 84
- The Last Supper, 86
- The Garden of Gethsemane, 88
- The Crucifixion, 90
- The Resurrection, 92
- The Ascension, 94

New Testament

cloud

sun

lemur

The
Creation Story

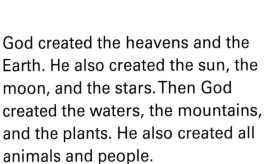

God created the heavens and the Earth. He also created the sun, the moon, and the stars. Then God created the waters, the mountains, and the plants. He also created all animals and people.

parrot

tree

tiger

hippopotamus

beaver

Adam and Eve

Adam and Eve lived in a beautiful garden. One day, a serpent told them to eat the fruit that God had forbidden them to eat. Adam and Eve disobeyed God. When God saw this, he responded by banishing them from the garden.

serpent

apple

leaf

pig

kangaroo

deer

lemon

orange

hammer

wolf

Building the **Ark**

plank of wood

When God saw how wicked people had become, he found one good man named Noah. God told Noah to build a giant ship called an ark, because God was going to flood the Earth to punish the wicked people. God told Noah to put two of every animal on the ark.

nail

crocodile

seal

bear

saw

The Great **Flood**

It rained hard and nonstop for 40 days. Noah and his family and the pairs of animals were all safe on the ark. When the Earth dried again, they left the ark and saw a rainbow, a sign of God's promise.

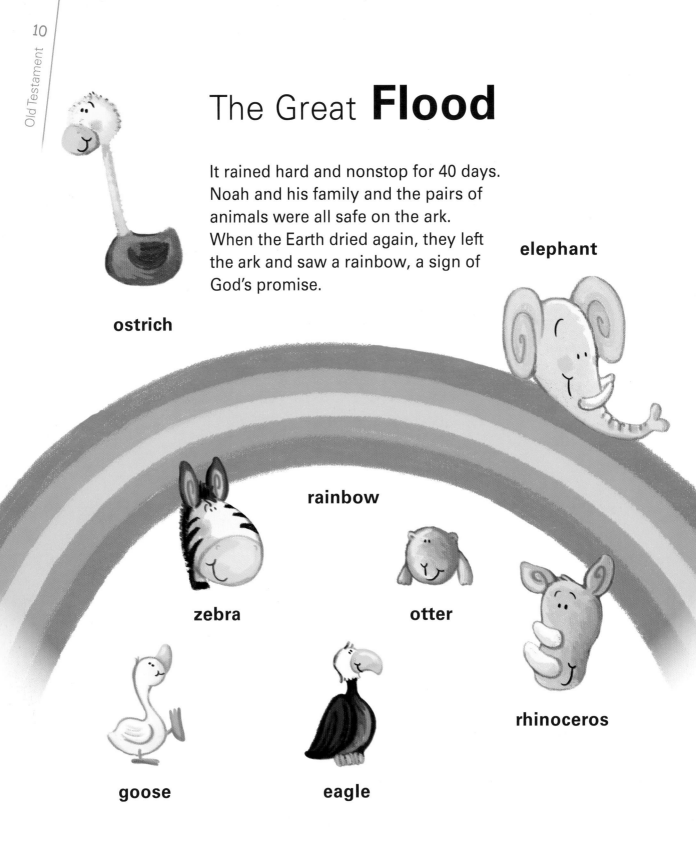

ostrich

elephant

rainbow

zebra

otter

goose

eagle

rhinoceros

bird

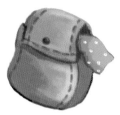

saddle bag

skirt

Abraham and Sarah

Abraham and Sarah loved God very much. One day, God asked them to move to a faraway place. They moved with their sheep and goats to the place God had told them.

sheep

donkey

goat

Isaac

Abraham and Sarah were very old and did not have any children. One night, while Abraham was looking at the stars, God told him that he would have descendants as numerous as the stars. One year later, their son Isaac was born.

stars

owl

dragonfly

firefly

moon

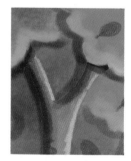

lantern

belt

tree branch

snail

stone

Jacob's
Dream

Isaac and his wife, Rebekah, had two sons, Esau and Jacob. One night, Jacob had a dream in which God told him, "I promise I will never leave you."

leather pouch

trunk

lizard

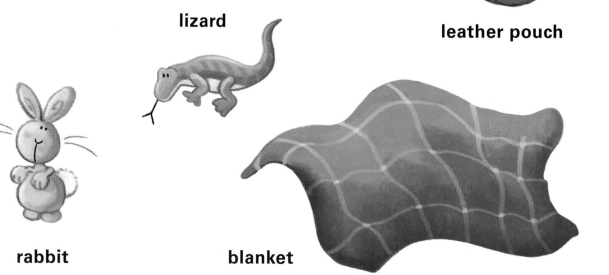

rabbit

blanket

Jacob's **Children**

Jacob had many children, and although he loved all of them very much, Joseph was his favorite.

grapes

hedgehog

spiderweb

pear

window

spider

door

fruit tree

nest

grain

grasshopper

Joseph

cat

One day, Jacob gave his son Joseph a beautiful coat of many colors. When Joseph's brothers and sister saw it, they were very jealous.

chick

ladybug

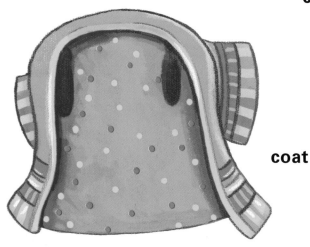

coat

hen

Joseph and His Brothers

palm tree

Joseph's brothers were very angry. One day, they grabbed Joseph, took his coat, and sold him to traders headed for Egypt, a faraway country.

sack

rope

butterfly

camel

tent

cactus

Joseph in
Egypt

Joseph could explain the meanings of dreams. The pharaoh, the king of Egypt, called for Joseph to explain his dreams. Joseph advised the pharaoh, and the pharaoh always followed his advice.

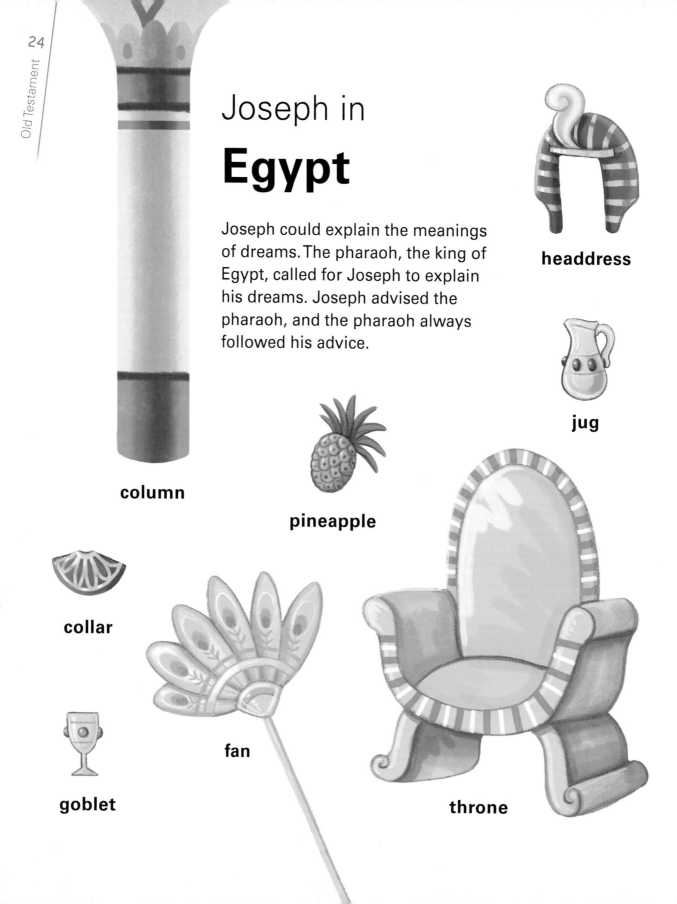

headdress

jug

column

pineapple

collar

fan

goblet

throne

The **Israelites** in Egypt

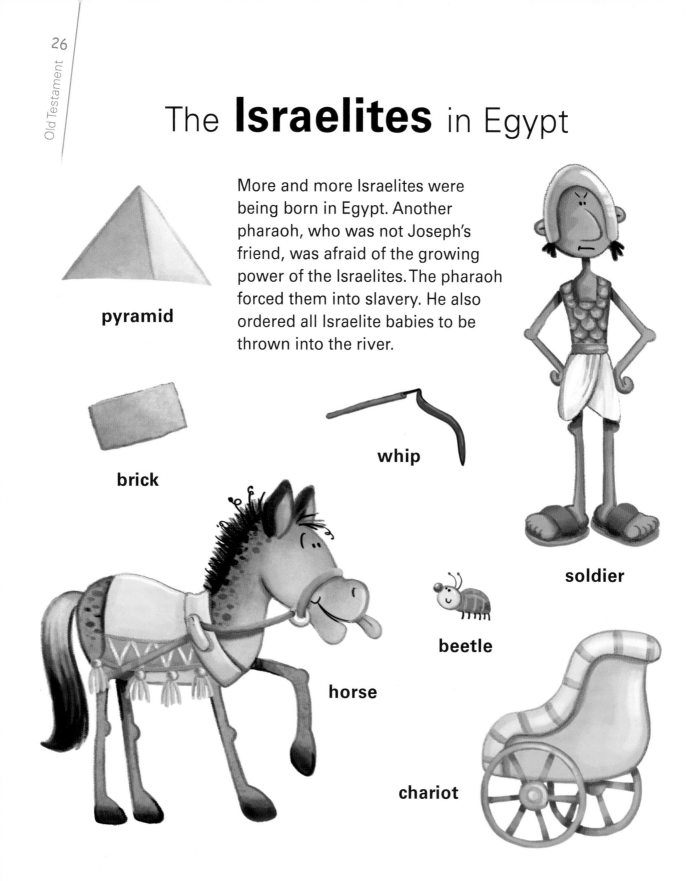

More and more Israelites were being born in Egypt. Another pharaoh, who was not Joseph's friend, was afraid of the growing power of the Israelites. The pharaoh forced them into slavery. He also ordered all Israelite babies to be thrown into the river.

pyramid

brick

whip

soldier

horse

beetle

chariot

basket

water lily

Moses

To save her son, an Israelite mother made a basket from reeds and put her son in it. She let the basket float down the river. The pharaoh's daughter found the baby and took very good care of him. She named him Moses.

sheet

frog

dragonfly

duck

reed

cuff

The Burning **Bush**

wool

When Moses grew up, he went into the desert because he had upset the pharaoh. He saw a burning bush there, and a voice said: "Moses, return to Egypt and tell the pharaoh to set the Israelites free."

ant

bell

weeds

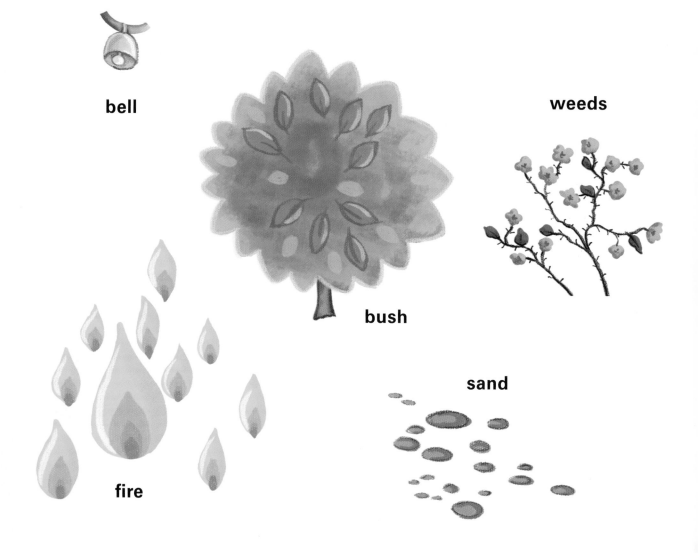

bush

sand

fire

carrot

cow

Leaving
Egypt

At first, the pharaoh did not want to let the Israelites leave Egypt. God grew angry with him and sent down many plagues.

waterskin

Finally, the pharaoh let the Israelites leave, and Moses guided them toward the Promised Land.

cheese

wing

pig

rooster

bags

A **Path** Through the Water

seagull

crab

During their journey to the Promised Land, the Israelites came to a big sea. They could not cross it because they did not have any boats.

God sent a very strong wind. The wind parted the waters and made a path for them through the sea. Then they could safely cross it.

seahorse

clay pot

beard

braid

octopus

wind

bowl

stool

mouse

Manna
from Heaven

The Israelites were traveling through the desert and were thirsty and hungry. God sent them bread from heaven that fell down like rain. This bread was called "manna."

fork

manna

turkey

blouse

stick

The Ten
Commandments

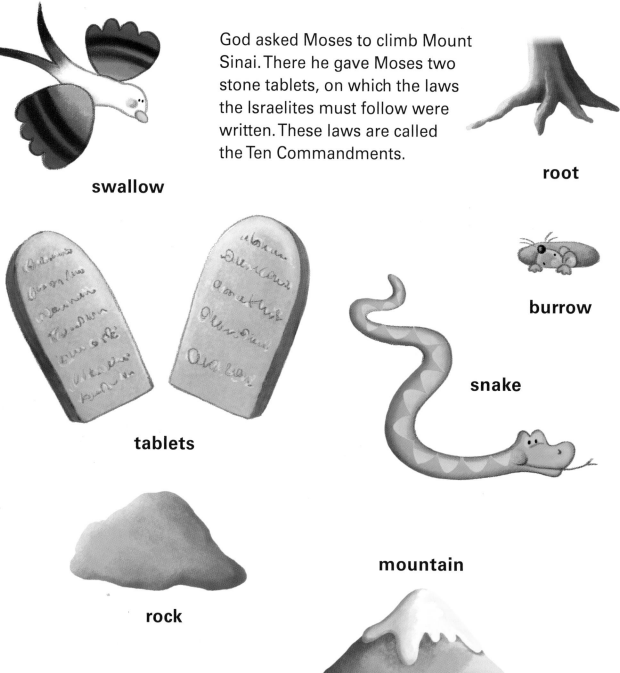

God asked Moses to climb Mount Sinai. There he gave Moses two stone tablets, on which the laws the Israelites must follow were written. These laws are called the Ten Commandments.

swallow

root

burrow

snake

tablets

mountain

rock

garland

chest

The **Ark** of the Covenant

The Israelites built a beautiful ark and put the stone tablets with the Ten Commandments inside it. When they stopped to rest during their journey through the desert, they put the ark in a tent and prayed to God before it.

menorah

flower

cushion

curtain

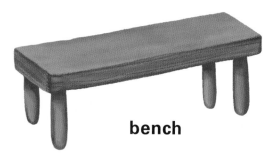

bench

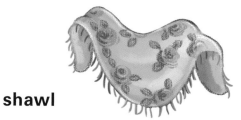

shawl

David and Goliath

sword

Many years later, a young shepherd
named David fought a giant named
Goliath. David defeated him and
eventually was proclaimed king.
God was always at David's side.

wheel

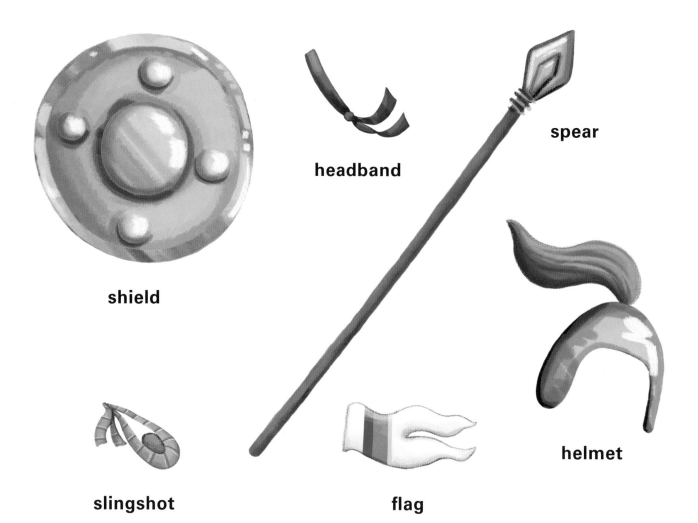

shield

headband

spear

slingshot

flag

helmet

flute

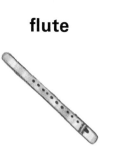

drum

painting

King David
in Jerusalem

trumpet

David picked Jerusalem as the capital of his kingdom. The Ark of the Covenant was moved there, and King David often sang and danced around it. He wanted to build a temple to hold the Ark, but he was not able.

carpet

harp

chest

pot

Solomon,
the Wise King

tray

vase

When David died, his son Solomon became the new king of Israel. King Solomon built the temple that his father had wanted. Solomon loved God very much and only asked him for wisdom to govern his people.

strawberry

shelf

ring

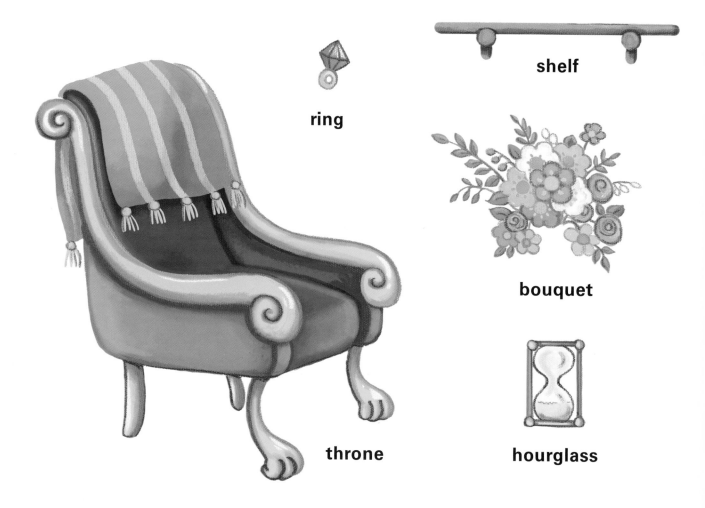

bouquet

throne

hourglass

bolt

Daniel and
the Lions

lion

fly

Daniel was a prophet who loved God. For this reason, one day he was punished by the king and thrown into a den with lions. Daniel asked God to help him, and the lions did not hurt him.

straw

gate

claw

bone

tail

The Prophet **Jonah**

lightning

barrel

Jonah refused God's call to serve as a prophet. While on a boat, a big storm came up. Jonah fell into the sea, and a big fish swallowed him. Then he asked the Lord's forgiveness. Jonah was freed and went on to be a great prophet.

anchor

sea star

boat

whale

wave

pumpkin

chair

The Prophet
Isaiah

peanuts

Isaiah was also a very important prophet.
One day, he announced that a young woman would have a baby who would become King and be the Savior of Israel.

paper

chipmunk

desk

fireplace

An **Angel** Visits Mary

Mary was a young woman who lived in Nazareth. One day, God sent an angel who told her: "Rejoice, Mary! You will have a son, and you will name him Jesus. He will be the Savior."

sunflower

hair bow

rocking chair

balls of wool

scarf

dog

angel

lid

milk jug

wooden spoon

towel

Mary Visits **Elizabeth**

Mary went to visit her cousin Elizabeth, who was also pregnant. Elizabeth's baby would become John the Baptist. When he was older, John the Baptist would tell the people that Jesus was the Savior.

charcoal

apron

scales

pot

horseshoe

firewood

The Birth of
Jesus

Mary and her husband, Joseph, traveled to Bethlehem. When they arrived, they had to stay in a stable because all the inns were full. Their son Jesus was born that night.

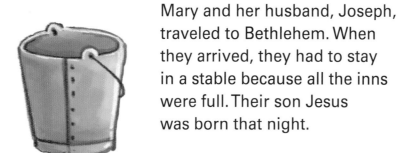

bucket

wheelbarrow

rake

turtle

ox

watering can

egg

potato

acorn

tomato

The Adoration
of the **Shepherds**

shepherd

In the countryside near Bethlehem, several shepherds were watching over their flock. An angel suddenly appeared and told them: "Today in Bethlehem the Messiah—the Savior—is born." The shepherds immediately traveled to Bethlehem to find and worship the baby Jesus.

lettuce

honey

pine

crown

The
Magi

brooch

After Jesus was born, three Magi saw a bright star in the sky. They followed it, and it led them to Jesus. When they saw the child, they worshiped him and gave him gifts of gold, frankincense, and myrrh.

key

bright star

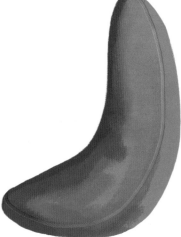

cape

cradle

shoe

rattle

books

side table

plant

Jesus in the
Temple

button

When Jesus was 12 years old, his parents took him to the Temple in Jerusalem. Later, as they were heading home, Joseph and Mary realized that Jesus was not with them. They returned quickly to the Temple and found him there, talking to the elders.

priest

altar

The **Baptism** of Jesus

John the Baptist prepared people to welcome Jesus as their Savior by baptizing them. One day, Jesus asked John to baptize him. When he did, a voice boomed from the sky and said: "This is my beloved Son."

coconut

dove

river

clover

chameleon

tadpole

swan

camel hair tunic

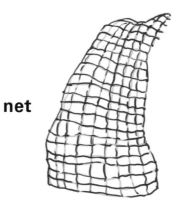

net

fish hook

Jesus'
Disciples

After Jesus grew up, he taught people who God is and how much he loves us all.

To help him in his mission, Jesus chose 12 men and called them his disciples.

sail

shell

oar

fisherman

rod

The **Wedding** at Cana

daisies

Mary, Jesus, and his disciples were invited to a wedding. During the reception, the wine ran out. Jesus miraculously changed six jugs of water into a delicious wine. This was Jesus' first miracle.

glass

mug

plate

soup tureen

raspberry

cake

ladle

Multiplication of the **Loaves** and **Fish**

loaf

Many people came to Jesus to listen to his stories. One afternoon, the people listening to him were hungry and did not have any food. Jesus took five loaves of bread and two fish and multiplied them, so everyone could eat.

mustache

bag

ponytail

fish

cicada

basket

bandage

road

hatchet

pitchfork

The **Parables**

cart

Jesus went from town to town telling stories that taught important lessons. These stories were called parables. They explained how God loved the people and always forgave them.

mill

bridge

corn

wheat

The **Lost Sheep**

bee

One time, Jesus told his followers a parable about a shepherd who lost a sheep from his flock and went to search for it. When he found the lost sheep, the shepherd was so happy that he told all his friends.

lamb

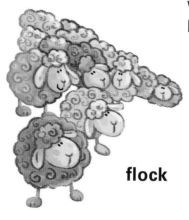

flock

sheepskin tunic

bale of hay

vegetable garden

puddle

beehive

cherry

banana

kite

Jesus and the
Children

worm

One afternoon, parents took their children to Jesus so he could bless them. The disciples told them not to bother Jesus. Jesus scolded the disciples for saying this. Jesus said, "Let the children come to me."

pocket

ball

doll

apricot

sculpture

ball of yarn

Triumphal Entry into
Jerusalem

Jesus and his disciples went to Jerusalem to celebrate Passover. Jesus entered the city riding a donkey, and the people welcomed him like a king. They waved palm and olive branches while crying out, "Blessed is he who comes in the name of the Lord!"

ivy

palm

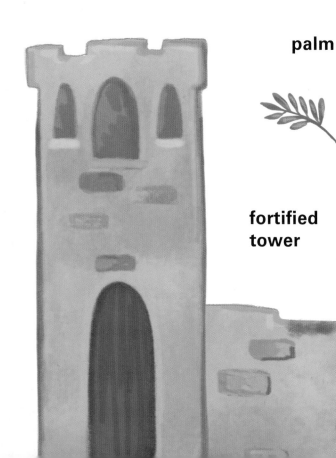

fortified tower

reins

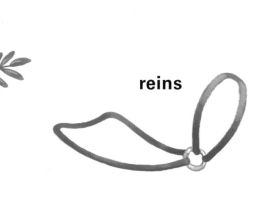

wall

ceiling

Judas's
Betrayal

cockroach

The chief priests did not like Jesus. One day, they gave money to Judas Iscariot, one of Jesus' disciples, so that he would tell them where they could find and arrest Jesus.

tile

coins

hook

lamp

trunk

The **Last Supper**

wine

Jesus wanted to celebrate the Passover feast with his disciples. This meal is called the Last Supper. Jesus gave thanks to God. He gave his Body and Blood to all people. Jesus was very sad because he knew that Judas was going to betray him.

broom

bread

napkin

fruit platter

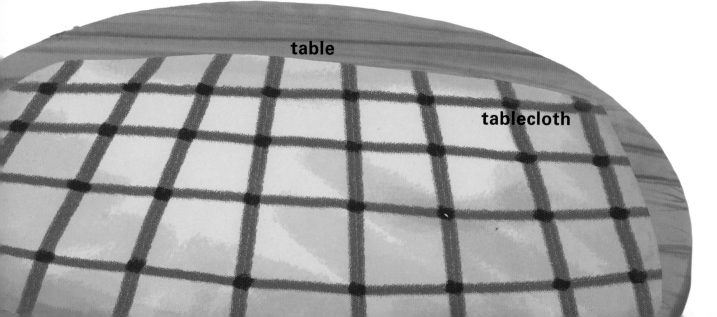

table

tablecloth

olives

torch

The Garden of
Gethsemane

raven

When the meal was over, Jesus
and his disciples went to pray on
the Mount of Olives.

arrow

Suddenly, Judas arrived with
soldiers bearing swords and clubs.
They grabbed Jesus and took him
to the governor, Pontius Pilate.

fence

armor

bow

olive tree

The **Crucifixion**

bat

Pontius Pilate condemned Jesus to death. He had Jesus taken to Calvary and crucified.

Among others, John and Jesus' mother, Mary, were close to the cross when Jesus died.

tear

cross

town

hood

lavender

pine tree

jar

mushrooms

The **Resurrection**

On the Friday that Jesus died, his friends buried him in a cave. On Sunday morning, when several women went to visit him, they saw that the rock over the entrance was no longer there. An angel told them that Jesus had risen.

feather

rose

tulip

centipede

cave

The **Ascension**

After his Resurrection, Jesus appeared to his disciples several times. After 40 days, he ascended into heaven. Jesus sent the Holy Spirit and soon many people were baptized as believers in Jesus as our Savior.

ladder

hinge

doorknob

rays of light

shutters

scorpion

tub

LOYOLA PRESS.

3441 N. Ashland Avenue
Chicago, Illinois 60657
(800) 621-1008
www.loyolapress.com

Text: Elisenda Castells

Illustration: Gabrielle Murphy

Design and layout: Estudi Guasch, S.L.

Originally published as *Biblia busca i troba.*

© Gemser Publications, S.L. 2019

El Castell, 38   08329 Teià (Barcelona, Spain)

www.mercedesros.com

Published in the United States in 2020 by Loyola Press.

ISBN: 978-0-8294-4955-6

Library of Congress Control Number: 2019945560

Printed in China